TAKING MY TURN

A Musical
from the writings of people in their prime.

Conceived and Adapted by
Robert H. Livingston

Music by Gary William Friedman
Lyrics by Will Holt

Arrangements and Orchestrations
by GARY WILLIAM FRIEDMAN
Conceived and Adapted
by ROBERT H. LIVINGSTON
from the writings of the following people in their prime:

Elise Brosnan	Will Holt	Janet Neuman
Diana Collins	Abe Janowitz	Anna Popkin
Diana Ellman	Anna Kainen	Susan Rifkin
Frances Feldman	Gertrude Weil Klein	Gertrude Schleier
Morton & Elise	Bobo Lewis	Rose Schulman
Goldman	Mary Lipke	Ida Schiffman
Pauline Goodman	Sara Lipsky	Bea Smith
Ethel Green	Dorothy Livingston	Rose Snyderman
Lillian Hendel	Esta Wolff March	Bertha Wohl
Don Herold	Ruth Mooney	Members of JASA

Original New York Production directed by
ROBERT H. LIVINGSTON

Amateurs wishing to arrange for the production of TAKING MY TURN must make application to SAMUEL FRENCH, INC., at 45 West 25th Street, New York, N.Y. 10010, giving the following particulars:

(1) The name of the town and theatre or hall in which it is proposed to give the production.
(2) The maximum seating capacity of the theatre or hall.
(3) Scale of ticket prices.
(4) The number of performances it is intended to give, and the dates thereof.
(5) Indicate whether you will use an orchestration or simply a piano.

Upon receipt of these particulars SAMUEL FRENCH, INC., will quote terms and availability.

Stock royalty quoted on application to SAMUEL FRENCH, INC., 45 West 25th Street, New York, N.Y. 10010.

For all other rights than those stipulated above apply to SAMUEL FRENCH, INC., 45 West 25th Street, New York, N.Y. 10010.

An orchestration consisting of:

Piano Conductor
Bass
Percussion
Reed
Trombone
Horn

will be loaned two months prior to the production ONLY on receipt of the royalty quoted for all performances, the rental fee and a refundable deposit. The deposit will be refunded on the safe return to SAMUEL FRENCH, INC. of all materials loaned for the production.

CARH

Printed in U.S.A.

ISBN 0 573 68127 9

IMPORTANT ADVERTISING NOTE

Producers of *TAKING MY TURN* are hereby notified that the Authors of the play must receive billing as sole Authors in any and all advertising and publicity issued in connection with amateur, stock or professional production of the Play. Said billing shall appear in but not be limited to all houseboards, advertisements, marquees, displays, posters, throwaways, circulars, announcements, and whenever and wherever the title of the Play appears. The Authors' billing, respectively, shall be on a separate line upon which no other matter appears, and shall follow the title of the Play. The names of the Authors shall be at least fifty percent (50%) of the size of type and prominence of the title of the Play. Billing must appear in the following form:

(Name of Producer)
presents
TAKING MY TURN
Music by GARY WILLIAM FRIEDMAN
Lyrics by WILL HOLT
Conceived & Adapted by ROBERT H. LIVINGSTON

IMPORTANT BILLING NOTE

The following notice must appear in all programs for productions of *TAKING MY TURN:*

TAKING MY TURN has been conceived and adapted by Robert Livingston from the writings of the following people in their prime:

Elise Brosnan	Will Holt	Janet Neuman
Diana Collins	Abe Janowitz	Anna Popkin
Diana Ellman	Anna Kainen	Susan Rifkin
Frances Feldman	Gertrude Weil Klein	Gertrude Schleier
Morton & Elise	Bobo Lewis	Rose Schulman
Goldman	Mary Lipke	Ida Schiffman
Pauline Goodman	Sara Lipsky	Bea Smith
Ethel Green	Dorothy Livingston	Rose Snyderman
Lillian Hendel	Esta Wolff March	Bertha Wohl
Don Herold	Ruth Mooney	Members of JASA

Original New York Production directed by
ROBERT H. LIVINGSTON

entermedia theatre

Under the Direction of

Joseph Asaro
Executive Director

David Secter
Creative Director

Richard Seader   Joanne Cummings
Maurice Levine   Arleen & Anthony Kane
Sonny Fox   Sally Sears

present

TAKING MY TURN

A Musical Celebration
Based on writings by people in their prime

Music By
Gary William Friedman

Lyrics By
Will Holt

With

Margaret Whiting	**Marni Nixon**	**Sheila Smith**	**Cissy Houston**
Tiger Haynes	**Victor Griffin**	**Mace Barrett**	**Ted Thurston**

Musical Direction by Barry Levitt

Arrangements and Orchestration by Gary William Friedman

Scenery By
Clarke Dunham

Lighting By
David F. Segal

Costumes By
Judith Dolan

Casting by Hughes Moss

Musical Staging By Douglas Norwick

Conceived and Directed by
Robert H. Livingston

4

CAST

(in order of appearance)

Eric	MACE BARRETT
Edna	MARNI NIXON
John	VICTOR GRIFFIN
Helen	CISSY HOUSTON
Charles	TIGER HAYNES
Dorothy	MARGARET WHITING
Benjamin	TED THURSTON
Janet	SHEILA SMITH

The play takes place during the course of one year...this year

THERE WILL BE ONE 15 MINUTE INTERMISSION

UNDERSTUDIES

Understudies never substitute for listed players unless a specific announcement
of the appearance is made at the time of the performance.

For Eric and Charles — Irving Barnes; for John and Benjamin — Edward Penn; for Edna, Helen,
Dorothy and Janet — Sis Clark.

MUSICAL NUMBERS
ACT I — Spring-Summer

THIS IS MY SONG	The Company
SOMEBODY ELSE, NOT ME	The Company
FINE FOR THE SHAPE I'M IN	Dorothy, Edna, Helen
TWO OF ME	Janet
JANET GET UP	The Company
I LIKE IT	The Company
I NEVER MADE MONEY FROM MUSIC	Charles
VIVALDI	Edna and Company
DO YOU REMEMBER?	Ben and Company
IN APRIL	Dorothy
PICK MORE DAISIES	The Company

ACT II — Fall-Winter

TAKING OUR TURN	The Company
SWEET LONGINGS	Janet and Company
I AM NOT OLD	Helen
DO YOU REMEMBER?(reprise)	Ben and Company
THE KITE	John
GOOD LUCK TO YOU	Eric and Company
IN THE HOUSE	Eric
SOMEBODY ELSE(reprise)	The Company
IT STILL ISN'T OVER	Ben and Dorothy
THIS IS MY SONG	The Company

BAND

BARRY LEVITT	Musical Director and Keyboards
RICHIE PRATT	Drums
RON McLURE	Bass
AL HUNT	Sax and Woodwinds
FRED GRIFFEN	French Horn
LARRY FARRELL	Trombone
PETER CALANDRA	Assistant to the Musical Director

Some of the material is based on the writings of the following people in their prime:

Elise Brosnan	Lillian Hendel	Sara Lipsky	Gertrude Schleier
Diana Collins	Don Herold	Dorothy Livingston	Rose Schulman
Diana Ellman	Abe Janowitz	Esta Wolff March	Ida Schiffman
Frances Feldman	Anna Kainen	Ruth Mooney	Bea Smith
Morton & Elise Goldman	Gertrude Weil Klein	Janet Neuman	Rose Snyderman
Pauline Goodman	Bobo Lewis	Anna Popkin	Bertha Wohl
Ethel Greene	Mary Lipke	Susan Rifkin	Members of JASA

TAKING MY TURN

TAKING MY TURN was first presented at The Entermedia Theatre in New York City. It opened on June 9, 1983 with the following cast. (see program on page 4.)

This musical was based on the writings of "people in their prime". The material was collected by Robert H. Livingston and the pieces that appear in the play were chosen from over 3,000 selections. There is no story, per se, but rather the show reflects various attitudes, feelings, experiences and ideas about growing older.

The cast includes eight people, four men and four women. One man should be black and one woman should be black. However, any ethnic mix is possible.

ERIC — a would-be writer who has been around the world often, sort of a philosopher-poet, a man of the street and the earth.

JOHN — a retired school teacher, eager to find something else to do with the rest of his years, does not quite have the courage.

CHARLES — a railroad steward, knows he missed an opportunity early in life when he chose the security of working for the railroads rather than a life in the world of music.

BENJAMIN — a lawyer, still active in his practice, has been writing letters to public figures for years, and is married to

DOROTHY — for years an activist and still out there fighting for causes. She and Ben lost a grown son.

HELEN — a physical therapist, mother and grandmother, who takes each new day as a challenge.

EDNA — a music teacher, just overcoming her timidity, daring to accept the romance and adventure that life offers.

JANET — a widow of two years, is at first a recluse, afraid to re-enter life on her own, and later a fine spirited, gracious woman of means.

The play takes place over the course of one year, beginning and ending at that time just before Spring. There is no "set", but there should be some levels to achieve variety and create interesting "pictures." Lively colors are important. Much should be done with lights for focus on various moments and, from time to time, to achieve isolation with each character. Two followspots are very useful. The play should be done without props. The actors should be dressed to look as if they just stepped out of life and entered the theatre. (no changes) Again, lively colors are important.

The actors should be directed to perform their speeches in three different styles; some speeches are *inner thoughts,* (which we "overhear"); some speeches are *dialogue,* in the traditional theatrical sense, characters speaking to one another; and some speeches are given directly to the audience in an interaction with them. Simplicity and honesty are the key words in achieving the strength and fiesty-ness of the work.

ROBERT H. LIVINGSTON

TAKING MY TURN

The cast includes eight people, four men and four women. One man should be black and one woman should be black. However, any ethnic mix is possible.

ERIC — a would-be writer who has been around the world often, sort of a philosopher-poet, a man of the street and the earth.

JOHN — a retired school teacher, eager to find something else to do with the rest of his years, does not quite have the courage.

CHARLES — a railroad steward, knows he missed an opportunity early in life when he chose the security of working for the railroads rather than a life in the world of music.

BENJAMIN — a lawyer, still active in his practice, has been writing letters to public figures for years, and is married to

DOROTHY — for years an activist and still out there fighting for causes. She and Ben lost a grown son.

HELEN — a physical therapist, mother and grandmother, who takes each new day as a challenge.

EDNA — a music teacher, just overcoming her timidity, daring to accept the romance and adventure that life offers.

JANET — a widow of two years, is at first a recluse, afraid to re-enter life on her own, and later a fine spirited, gracious woman of means.

The play takes place over the course of one year, beginning and ending at that time just before Spring. There is no "set", but there should be some levels to achieve variety and create interesting "pictures." Lively colors are important. Much should be done with lights for focus on various moments and, from time to time, to achieve isolation with each character. Two followspots are very useful. The play should be done without props. The actors should be dressed to look as if they just stepped out of life and entered the theatre. (no changes) Again, lively colors are important.

The actors should be directed to perform their speeches in three different styles; some speeches are *inner thoughts,* (which we "overhear"); some speeches are *dialogue,* in the traditional theatrical sense, characters speaking to one another; and some speeches are given directly to the audience in an interaction with them. Simplicity and honesty are the key words in achieving the strength and fiesty-ness of the work.

ROBERT H. LIVINGSTON

CAST OF CHARACTERS

ERIC
EDNA
JOHN
HELEN
CHARLES
DOROTHY
BENJAMIN
JANET

The action of the play takes place during the course of one year. . . .

MUSICAL NUMBERS

ACT I   SPRING—SUMMER

This is My Song
Somebody Else, Not Me
Fine for the Shape I'm In
Two of Me
Janet Get Up
I Like It
I Never Made Money from Music
Vivaldi
Do You Remember?
In April
Pick More Daisies

ACT II   FALL—WINTER

Taking Our Turn
Sweet Longings
I Am Not Old
Do You Remember? (reprise)
The Kite
Good Luck To You
In the House
Somebody Else (reprise)
It Still Isn't Over
This Is My Song

ACT I
SPRING – SUMMER

Taking My Turn

ACT I

FEBRUARY

(*MUSIC starts in the darkness. A single light comes up on ERIC, and then as each following person speaks, a single spotlight lights each one.*)

ERIC.
Dear Sirs: My essays on aging?
I'm delighted you want to use them in your new musical.
Two quick questions.
1. Do you want any more material?
2. Is there any money involved?
(*MUSIC escalates.*)

JOHN. A musical about aging? Won't that be depressing. Enclosed find two selections. (*MUSIC escalates again.*)

DOROTHY. I approve of your project but for God's sake, don't kill it with kindness. (*MUSIC escalates again.*)

EDNA. My contribution? Two short poems.

HELEN. Old is fifteen years from now.

BENJAMIN.
Growing old is a pain in the ass.
Signed, yours sincerely. . . .
(*MUSIC stops.*)

CHARLES. When I was a kid, the grown-ups said, "Hush, wait your turn." And when I was grown up, the kids were doing all the talking. At last, is it finally *my turn?* (*MUSIC changes.*)

THIS IS MY SONG

EDNA.
ONCE AGAIN TO FEEL THE THRILL
OF APRIL RISING ON THE HILL
HELEN.
ONCE AGAIN TO KNOW THE PAIN
AND TASTE THE JOYS OF LOVE AGAIN
CHARLES AND DOROTHY.
ONCE AGAIN TO FEAST UPON
THE PLEASURES THAT HAD ALL BUT GONE

ALL.
SPRING IS HEAVEN'S GIFT TO MEN
TO SAY IT ALL BEGINS AGAIN
THIS IS MY SONG
THIS IS MY NEW BEGINNING
THIS IS MY SONG
PERHAPS MY FINAL FLING
THIS IS MY SONG
AND IF I WANT TO SING IT
    BENJAMIN.
WHO'S GONNA STOP ME
IF I START TO SING!
    ALL.
THIS IS MY SONG
THIS IS MY NEW BEGINNING
THIS IS MY SONG
I NEVER SANG BEFORE

THIS IS MY SONG
AND IF I WANT TO SING IT
THIS IS MY SONG
I'M GONNA SING SOME MORE.

THIS IS MY SONG
THIS IS MY NEW BEGINNING
THIS IS MY SONG
I NEVER SANG BEFORE
THIS IS MY SONG
AND IF I WANT TO SING IT
THIS IS MY SONG
I'M GONNA SING SOME MORE

THIS IS MY SONG
THIS IS MY NEW BEGINNING
THIS IS MY SONG
PERHAPS MY FINAL FLING
THIS IS MY SONG
AND IF I WANT TO SING IT
WHO'S GONNA STOP ME
IF I START TO SING!
(*feeling a unity*)
THIS IS MY SONG!
THIS IS MY NEW BEGINNING!

THIS IS MY SONG!
PERHAPS MY FINAL FLING!
THIS IS MY SONG
SO PEOPLE, LISTEN TO ME SING!

JANET. My thoughts on aging? You'll find only anger here.
My husband died two years ago — just when I needed him most.
Now I just want to be left alone.

EDNA, HELEN, AND DOROTHY.
SOON ENOUGH WE FEEL THE CHILL
OF AUTUMN RISING ON THE HILL

WOMEN.
SOON ENOUGH WE KNOW WE MIGHT
NOT QUITE RECOVER FROM THE NIGHT

MEN.
SOON ENOUGH WILL COME THE TIME
YOUR HAND WILL SLIP AWAY FROM MINE

ALL.
MAYBE WHAT WE CALLED THE END
MAY BE BEGINNING ONCE AGAIN!

THIS IS MY SONG
THIS IS MY NEW BEGINNING
THIS IS MY SONG
I NEVER SANG BEFORE
THIS IS MY SONG
AND IF I WANT TO SING IT
THIS IS MY SONG
I'M GONNA SING SOME MORE

THIS IS MY SONG
THIS IS MY NEW BEGINNING
THIS IS MY SONG
PERHAPS MY FINAL FLING
THIS IS MY SONG
AND IF I WANT TO SING IT
WHO'S GONNA STOP ME
IF I START TO SING!
(*feeling a unity*)
THIS IS MY SONG!
THIS IS MY NEW BEGINNING!
THIS IS MY SONG!

EDNA. A musical based on the writings of older people — what
for? What kind of people would they be? (*looks over shoulder*)

I'm not sure I qualify here. After all I don't think of myself as being that old.

DOROTHY, ERIC, BEN. Who does?

EDNA. And what kind of poetry and stories would they do?

HELEN. (*giving an example*)

When I first got my Half-Fare pass
I wouldn't use it in front of a friend.
Now I thrust my card at the bus driver
and glow to his accolade
"Lady, you don't look it!"

JOHN. I was retired — after thirty-one years. I miss teaching — school — classes. Even the students. Now I have so much time on my hands, I'm not sure what to do with it.

BENJAMIN. It's true. There just might be a conspiracy against aging. It's worth speaking up about.

To the Editor
The New York Times
Dear Sir:
I am replying to your article in last Sunday's Magazine Section entitled "A Life of Leisure."
I am still the senior partner in my own law firm and a better damn trial lawyer than most men half my age.

DOROTHY. Our kids tried talking us into living in Florida.

BENJAMIN. That's right. They did.

DOROTHY.

But I feel so alive here. As for Florida . . . you have to be a human orange to live there!

I once sold apples on the street in the bitter cold
When my nose would freeze
Took a job in Macy's basement
Peeling potatoes — with two graduate degrees
And went to jail for worthy causes . . .

I was marching then, and I'm still marching!

CHARLES. I remember once passing a sandlot where some boys were playing baseball. The outfielder missed a pop-fly and the ball came right toward me. One of the kids shouted, "Hey, mister, would ya get the ball?" And I turned around to see who "Mister" was. "Mister" was *me*. (*insert MUSIC under*) I was only twenty-eight at the time, but "Mister" made me feel old.

SOMEBODY ELSE, NOT ME

ERIC.
WHERE DID IT START?

HOW DID IT HAPPEN?
WHEN DID LIFE TURN THE PAGE?

WAS I AWAKE
OR WAS I CAUGHT NAPPING
WHEN I BEGAN TO AGE?

WHO'S GETTING OLD?
WHO'S GETTING OLDER
WHOSE IS THE FACE I SEE

WHAT A SURPRISE!
I MUST BE MISTAKEN!
THAT'S SOMEBODY ELSE, NOT ME.
   ERIC AND HELEN.
SOMEBODY ELSE, SOMEBODY OTHER
NO ONE I KNOW
SOMEBODY ELSE. SOMEONE WHOSE AGE
IS STARTING TO SHOW
THAT'S SOMEBODY ELSE — NOT ME!
   JOHN.
SOMEONE WHO'S REACHING THAT RESTLESS STAGE
THAT'S SOMEBODY ELSE, NOT ME.
   JANET.
SOMEONE WHO SITS
IN A SILENT RAGE
THAT'S SOMEBODY ELSE, NOT ME
   JOHN, BEN, DOROTHY, ERIC.
ALL THOSE WE KNOW
WITH NOWHERE TO GO
WITH THEIR HONORS AND THEIR DEGREES
   JOHN, BEN, DOROTHY, ERIC, HELEN.
PUT ON THE SHELF
PUT OUT TO PASTURE
PUT ON THE ICE TO FREEZE
   ALL.
THAT'S SOMEBODY ELSE, SOMEBODY OTHER
NO ONE I KNOW
SOMEBODY ELSE. SOMEONE WHOSE AGE
IS STARTING TO SHOW
THAT'S SOMEBODY ELSE, NOT ME
   BEN, DOROTHY, HELEN.
ONE SIGN OF AGE
WE ALL HAVE DISCOVERED

LOOKING AROUND TODAY
ALL OF A SUDDEN
ALL OF OUR CHILDREN
HAVE GOTTEN SO OLD AND GREY
    ALL.
THAT'S SOMEBODY ELSE
SOMEBODY OTHER
NO ONE I KNOW
SOMEBODY ELSE
SOMEONE WHOSE AGE
IS STARTING TO SHOW
THAT'S SOMEBODY ELSE,
    JANET.
NOT ME . . .
    CHARLES. (*singing*)
IF OLD IS PART OF ANOTHER COUNTRY
WHO DREW THE BOUNDARY LINE?
    ALL.
IF OLD IS PART OF ANOTHER COUNTRY
WHO DREW THE BOUNDARY LINE?

SOMEBODY ELSE!
SOMEBODY OTHER!
NO ONE I SEE!
COULD IT BE US?
COULD IT BE YOU?
COULD IT BE ME?

THAT'S SOMEBODY ELSE!

MARCH

ERIC. I never thought about being old—until there I was—surprised by time. Like a kid caught unprepared for his final exams.

JOHN. Let me tell you something. Schools don't prepare you for that.

BENJAMIN. Old is the time of life when you know all the answers and nobody asks you the questions.

CHARLES. Oh, no, it's a bonus baby; you get a second chance at life.

HELEN. You got to look for new things to do. See the fun in life.

DOROTHY. Age doesn't make you boring. Boring makes you boring!

JANET. My! Everyone has such definite opinions!

EDNA. Yes, isn't it wonderful?

ERIC. I've begun to notice changes. Changes in me, in my body. Little aches and pains.

JOHN.
Well, I'd trade the wisdom
That comes with age
For a body that's still on the go.

HELEN. My game is physical therapy. Aches and pains are just another part of life—like teenage acne. No need to get upset about it.

CHARLES. Just a minute. If I had known I was going to live this long, I would have taken better care of myself.

HELEN. And that means exercise.

EDNA. And that means work.

DOROTHY. And that means smile, even though it hurts your face.

FINE FOR THE SHAPE I'M IN

DOROTHY, EDNA, HELEN.
I'M
JUST AS HEALTHY AS I CAN BE
THERE AIN'T NOTHING WRONG THE MATTER
   WITH ME
I'M FINE—FOR THE SHAPE I'M IN.

AND OVERLOOK ALL TENDENCIES
TO HUFF AND PUFF AND WHEEZE AND SNEEZE
I'M FINE—FOR THE SHAPE I'M IN.

O THERE ARE ACHES AND THERE IS PAIN
AND I ALWAYS KNOW WHEN IT'S GONNA RAIN
CAUSE MY ELBOW ACTS LIKE A WEATHER VANE
BUT I DON'T COMPLAIN
FOR THE ONE THING NO ONE WANTS TO KNOW
WHEN THEY SAY "HOW ARE YA?" AND MEAN "HELLO"
IS JUST WHAT KIND OF SHAPE YOU'RE IN.

HELEN.
ARCH SUPPORTS SUPPORT MY FEET
IT TAKES ME HOURS TO CROSS THE STREET
I CAN'T STAND COLD AND I CAN'T GET HEAT
BUT I STILL REPEAT

HELEN, EDNA, DOROTHY.
I MAY BE LIVING ON ASPIRIN

BUT I MAKE DAMN SURE I SAY WITH A GRIN
I'M FINE—FOR THE SHAPE I'M IN.

HELEN. A visit to the doctor!

DOROTHY. The Doctor. "Well, well—and how are we today?"

EDNA. (*the patient*) Doctor, I have this. . . ."

DOROTHY. "Mmmmm! Interesting!"

EDNA. ". . . And for the past couple of weeks I've noticed . . ."

DOROTHY. "Hmmmm. How nice."

EDNA. ". . . And when I open my eyes . . ."

DOROTHY. "That's very common with people your age."

EDNA. "And I'm having an affair with Robert Redford."

DOROTHY. "There's been a lot of *that* going around this year."

ALL.

WORST OF ALL IS BEING TOLD
WHEN YOU'RE GETTING ON AND YOU'RE GETTING
    OLD
"YOU'RE FINE! BETTER THAN YOU'VE EVER BEEN!"

WELL, OF COURSE I'M FINE AND OF COURSE I'LL LIVE

DOROTHY. Considering the alternative.

HELEN, EDNA, DOROTHY.

I'M FINE—FOR THE SHAPE I'M IN

DOROTHY.

I'M FINE

HELEN.

I'M FINE

EDNA.

I'M FINE

HELEN, EDNA, DOROTHY.

WE'RE FINE

I'M FINE
FOR THE SHAPE I'M IN.

ERIC.

Some people have always been able to laugh at themselves.
Some people grow old before their time.
My mother did.
She changed almost overnight
Into an old and embittered woman
I couldn't accept the fact
That she was giving up on life.
She was about the age I am now.
The neighbors said she was "failing".

It was hard to watch
I still don't understand it.

TWO OF ME

JANET.
TWO OF, TWO OF ME
WHY MUST I SEE
TWO OF, TWO OF ME
THE YOUNG GIRL I
USED TO, USED TO BE
SO WONDERFULLY FAIR

TWO OF, TWO OF ME
THE YOUNG GIRL I
USED TO, USED TO BE
—THE OLD WOMAN
STARING BACK AT ME
WHOM I CANNOT BEAR

WHY, WHY ANSWER QUESTIONS?
WHY STIR UP THE MIND?
WHY, WHY TALK OF TORMENTS
THAT I LEFT BEHIND?
WHY WANDER DOWN HALLWAYS
CORNERED BY PAIN
WHY, WHY BRING UP SORROWS
THAT CAN'T BE EXPLAINED?

RAGE IS A RAZOR THAT CUTS THROUGH STONE!
WHY IN GOD'S NAME CAN'T YOU LEAVE ME ALONE?

TWO OF, TWO OF ME
WHY MUST SHE KEEP
HAUNTING, HAUNTING ME
THE YOUNG GIRL I
USED TO, USED TO BE
THAT I WAS BEFORE

TWO OF, TWO OF ME
THE WOMAN I
USED TO, USED TO BE
THE YOUNG WIFE HE
USED TO, USED TO SEE
THAT HE DID ADORE

I ONCE HAD A LOVER
WHO LOVED ONLY ME
I ONCE HAD A LOVER
WHOSE LOVE SET ME FREE
I ONCE HAD A LOVER
WHOSE LOVE KEPT ME YOUNG
I ONCE HAD A LIFE!
AND NOW I HAVE NONE!

SHATTER THE MIRRORS AND UNDERSTAND!
I CANNOT BEAR TO SEE WHAT IS AT HAND

TWO OF, TWO OF ME
WHY MUST SHE KEEP
HAUNTING, HAUNTING ME
THE YOUNG GIRL I
USED TO, USED TO BE
THAT I WAS BEFORE . . .

THAT I AM NO MORE.
(*Janet is still alone.*)
   HELEN. (*without sentiment*)
Don't talk to *me* of loneliness
Even in my dreams
I am alone.
And when my dreams disturb me
I shove them in a Hefty bag
And leave them on the curb!
   ERIC.
I have lived alone for years
I like it . . .
(*MUSIC under*)
I'm not a hermit
I enjoy a hearty meal with friends
A good movie
Women
But music has become
My best companion
It can be a comfort
Or it can give you a lift.

(*EDNA has been tapping her feet in time to the music. Now she
   gets up.*)

   EDNA. When I was a girl, it was an unthinkable breach of etiquette to ask a gentleman to dance. I think I'm old enough, now. (*to ERIC*) I'd like to dance. . . .

(*ERIC obliges. Thank heavens it's a waltz and he manages well enough. The others watch. HELEN definitely approves, as she tells us. JANET remains apart, immobile.*)

HELEN. (*to the audience*) Contrary to what you think, dancing does not tire you! Dancing hardens the muscles and enables you to walk better! Grace, poise and confidence are all yours in return for learning to dance. Perhaps it adds up to longevity. Regardless. Do get on the floor and DANCE!

BENJAMIN. Right!

JANET GET UP

HELEN AND BENJAMIN.
JANET, GET UP
THE MUSIC IS PLAYING
THEY STARTED THE DANCE
AND THE SOUND IS SO SWEET

JANET, GET UP
DO YOU HEAR WHAT WE'RE SAYING
WE'RE SAYING, GET UP ON YOUR FEET!

COME ON, GET UP
GET OFF YOUR ROCKER!
GET UP AND GET GOIN'
AND REACH FOR A STAR

YOU GOT A SIDE
THAT YOU HAVEN'T BEEN SHOWIN'
WE WANT TO SEE
JUST WHO YOU ARE
ALL.
DANCING IS FUN!
DANCING IS HEALTHY!
DANCING IS GRACE
BREEDING AND POISE!

DANCING'S THE WALTZ
DANCING'S THE TANGO
DOROTHY.
DANCING'S A CHANCE
TO GET CLOSE TO THE BOYS

ALL.
JANET, GET UP
THE MUSIC IS PLAYING
THEY STARTED THE DANCE
AND THE SOUND IS SO SWEET

JANET, GET UP
DO YOU HEAR WHAT WE'RE SAYING
WE'RE SAYING, GET UP ON YOUR FEET!

JOHN.
DANCING'S A SNAP
DANCING'S A TONIC
DANCING'S A WONDERFUL, GLORIOUS TREAT!

DANCING IS SURE
PURE SELF EXPRESSION

ALL.
AND ALSO A CHANCE TO
GET UP OFF YOUR SEAT!

(*Dance interlude*)

ALL. (*softly*)
JANET YOU'RE UP!
THE MUSIC WAS PLAYING
YOU STARTED TO DANCE
TO THE SOUND OF THE BEAT
JANET, YOU'RE UP
AND EVERYONE'S SAYING—
THANK HEAVENS, YOU'RE UP ON YOUR FEET!

JANET, JANET, JANET

JANET, YOU'RE UP!

APRIL

DOROTHY.
I do not remember ever being a child,
A perfect little lady,
Yes, ma'm, no ma'm,
In Mary Janes and pig-tails,
Did you know me?

A young lady, Miss Weil,
In high school,

I had the lead in the class-day play,
I do not remember how I got the lead,
Did I audition,
Did my elocution teacher recommend me,
Was I the tallest girl in the class?
I played the Mother;
I have no idea what the play was about;
One line lingers,
— Mother, you look so funny wearing your hat with your apron
   on. I don't think I wore a hat. — did the audience laugh?
Who forgot to bring a hat?

My wedding day — a blank,
Except for one incident,
As we are slowly walking to the alter
My mother hisses in my ear, stand up straight,
I probably did, I don't remember, I wasn't there;

I read a lot — books —
I lived in the library,
When I could get away from home.

The Bitter Tea of General Yen —
I have absolutely no recollection of what that book was all
   about,
Or even whether I ever read it.

But all my life has been
Trying to forget
The Bitter Tea of General Yen.

(*The sun is shining brightly, it is that time just before the
   brilliance of summer. A faint tune is heard in the distance.
   [MUSIC cue 61 — underscore.]*)

ERIC. City sounds. When I was in the merchant marines, I was
thinking of becoming a writer. I loved to poke around the cities
of the world — Shanghai, London, Rio de Janeiro. I still think
about becoming a writer. And I still poke around the city streets.
What I love is the life there — new faces, shop windows beckon-
ing. There's never a street corner without its own kind of music.
And now, sometimes, danger.

   HELEN.
Weaving toward me on 14th Street,
This bright and beautiful day,
A young Hispanic,
Singing,

Pirouetting to the tempo of his tune,
Swinging his arms at the passersby
Who scatter out of his way like sheep;

Fingers crossed, I walk a straight line,
Briefly letting his eyes meet mine,
Hand brush hand,
Smile catch smile,
As he dances by.
You are beautiful, mama,
He sings out,
I love you;
Ever so softly, I reply,
Thank you, and go
On my way
Down 14th Street
On this bright and beautiful day!

MAY

(*In the distance, we hear the sound of bongo drums. [MUSIC under CII]*)

JOHN. The City is full of noise! I go into the park for a little peace and quiet . . . and then get bombarded by those hooligans with their stereos!

(*MUSIC— The bongo drums are louder.*)

I LIKE IT

CHARLES.
I LIKE IT

JOHN.
I DON'T

EDNA, HELEN.
I LIKE IT

JANET.
I DON'T

ERIC, DOROTHY.
I LIKE IT

BEN.
I DON'T

CHARLES, EDNA, HELEN,
ERIC, DOROTHY.

JOHN, BENJAMIN, JANET.

IT IS GETTING WARMER
AND THEY ARE GOING
  TO COME HERE
WITH THEIR MUSIC

                    THEY CALL IT MUSIC

PORTABLE TRANSISTORS
TURNED UP VERY, VERY
  HIGH
TO PLAY THEIR MUSIC

                    THEY CALL IT MUSIC

I LIKE IT

(*Dance interlude*)

                    THEY ARE GOING TO
                      COME HERE
                    THEY'LL BE CROWDING
                      UP THE BENCHES
                    WITH THEIR MUSIC

                    THEY CALL IT MUSIC

I LIKE IT

                    TURNED ON VERY HIGH
                    AND ALSO TURNED ON
                      VERY LOUD
                    TO PLAY THEIR MUSIC

                    THEY CALL IT MUSIC

YEH!

                    AND THEY WILL SING
                    AND THEY WILL DANCE
                    AND EVEN FORM A BAND
                    AND EVEN IF THEY'RE
                      SINGING WORDS
                    I UNDERSTAND
                    I STILL WON'T UNDER-
                      STAND

AND THEY WILL SING
AND THEY WILL DANCE

AND EVEN FORM A BAND
AND EVEN IF THEY'RE
  SINGING WORDS
I UNDERSTAND
I STILL WON'T UNDER-
  STAND

CHARLES, EDNA, ERIC,   JANET, BENJAMIN, JOHN.
HELEN, DOROTHY.

                              IT'S TOO LOUD
I LIKE IT
                              IT'S TOO LOUD
I LIKE IT
                              IT'S TOO LOUD
I LIKE IT
                              AND IT HURTS THE EARS
I LIKE IT
                              IT'S TOO MUCH
I LIKE IT
                              IT'S TOO MUCH
I LIKE IT
                              IT'S TOO MUCH
I LIKE IT
IT'S TOO MUCH   IT'S TOO MUCH

(*MUSIC seques.*)

I NEVER MADE MONEY FROM MUSIC

CHARLES.
I NEVER MADE MONEY FROM MUSIC
I NEVER MADE NOTHIN' BUT FUN
I NEVER MADE MONEY FROM MUSIC
AND MOSTLY I LIVED ON THE RUN

SATURDAY NIGHTS, DOWN AT THE GRANGE
MAN, IT WAS HOT
AND THEY'D THROW ME THEIR CHANGE
WHICH WOULD LAND IN A HAT BY MY FEET

AND I NEVER MADE MONEY FROM MUSIC
I ONCE BOUGHT A SECOND HAND CAR
THOUGH EVERYONE TOLD ME I COULD HAVE
I NEVER DID GO VERY FAR

FROM THOSE
SATURDAY NIGHTS, DOWN AT THE GRANGE
MAN, IT WAS HOT
AND THEY'D THROW ME THEIR CHANGE
WHICH WOULD LAND BY MY FEET

AND I PLAYED FOR THOSE SATURDAY DANCES
AND IT NEVER DID BOTHER ME NONE
THAT I NEVER MADE MONEY FROM MUSIC
'CAUSE I NEVER HAD NOTHIN' BUT FUN

NO, I NEVER MADE MONEY FROM MUSIC
BUT I NEVER HAD NOTHIN' BUT FUN.

JUNE

EDNA. I stay out late when there's something interesting to stay out for, like Shakespeare in the Park. All right, it's dangerous to stay out late at night. But what's the worst thing that could happen? You could be murdered. Then you'd stop living. But why stop living even before you're murdered?

VIVALDI

EDNA. (*singing*)
ON SUNDAYS IN THE PARK
YOU ARE AT A FIESTA
WALK THE WORLD OF SOUNDS
AND UNDER EVERY TREE
A FLUTE AND A RECORDER
AND GUITAR
WILL PLAY VIVALDI! VIVALDI! THERE YOU ARE

WHEN I HEARD THE SOUND
IT WAS LATE IN SPRING
THE MUSIC WITHIN ME
SAID TO ME—SING

I ADDED MY VOICE
TO ASTONISHED STARES
IF PEOPLE WERE MOCKING ME
I STILL DIDN'T CARE

I FELT SO ALIVE
WITH BLESSINGS ABOVE
AND SINGING VIVALDI
WITH LOVE
(*interlude*)
FOR MOST OF THE DAY
WE KEPT PLAYING ON
TILL FLUTE AND RECORDER
AND SUNLIGHT WERE GONE

VIVALDI RAN OFF
WHEN HE'D BROKEN A STRING
AND ONLY THE SONGBIRDS
CONTINUED TO SING

THE REST OF THE WORLD
SLIPPED INTO THE DARK
AND LEFT ME ALONE IN
DEEP — CENTRAL PARK.
(*interlude*)
    DOROTHY. Were you scared?
    EDNA. Yes . . . and no.
FOR I WAS ALIVE
IT WAS LATE IN SPRING
THE MUSIC WITHIN ME
SAID TO ME — SING!

THE WORLD DID RESOUND
WITH BLESSINGS ABOVE
ALL SINGING VIVALDI
    ALL.
VIVALDI! VIVALDI!

WITH
LOVE!

JULY

    BENJAMIN. You know, I've never understood why it's so important for older people *not* to live dangerously. I mean, after all, we've lived *most* of our lives, so who is better qualified to take risks?

CHARLES. I'll tell you what's dangerous. At night you could get mugged, but in the daytime, you could get run over by a bicycle.

JANET. Well, there's no place that's safe. At home, you could fall off a ladder. Outside, in mid-town Manhattan today you could just as easily get hit by a falling flower pot. Incidentally, I do not believe that all change is for the better. For instance, have you ever once referred to Sixth Avenue as Avenue of the Americas?

ERIC.
Where I grew up
There were no "underprivileged",
only poor — and very poor. . . .
We were poor.
We lived in a factory row house in Pittsburgh
My father made us bed-room slippers out of old felt hats —
My father.
We always had handkerchiefs.
"Blow" handkerchiefs and "show" handkerchiefs!
Remember?

JOHN. I remember New York City in the twenties, and thirties. What was it that created a nostalgia and an excitement? (*MUSIC under*) Was it the city with it's glamour or the world outside that held hope?

JANET. Smartly dressed women and mansions of the wealthy.

HELEN. The double-decker busses on Fifth Avenue where you could ride in the open air. . . .

ERIC. . . . the jelly apple man fixing the apple while you waited . . . (*MUSIC is brighter.*)

CHARLES. Was it the sound of the dance bands and the rehearsal halls along Broadway?

DOROTHY. It was the organ grinder man walking along talking to his little monkey . . .

BENJAMIN. . . . spats over your shoes and cigarette holders almost a foot long . . .

EDNA. . . . and leopard-skin coats, and dresses dripping with monkey fur.

ERIC. It was the old lady standing in front of the Roxy, selling gardenias or violets according to the season . . .

CHARLES. Well, that's all gone. . . .

ERIC. What?

CHARLES. The lady . . . The Roxy . . . and the gardenias, — all gone.

BENJAMIN.
To the Editor:
Dear Sir. . . .
Question!!!

DO YOU REMEMBER?

BENJAMIN.
DO YOU REMEMBER WHEN PEOPLE SAID "THANK YOU"?
DO YOU REMEMBER WHEN PEOPLE SAID "PLEASE"?
ERIC.
DO YOU REMEMBER POLITE CONVERSATION?
ERIC, BEN.
WHATEVER HAPPENED TO THESE?
EDNA.
A PHRASE LIKE "GOOD GRACIOUS"

BENJAMIN.
A WORD SUCH AS "PRETTY".
HELEN AND JANET.
WERE FRIENDS THAT WE LIVED WITH IN OUR NEIGHBORHOOD
BENJAMIN.
WHERE DID THEY GO TO — AND WHEN DID THEY LEAVE US?
AND OH, DID THEY LEAVE US FOR GOOD?
ALL.
"PRETTY" AND "SWEETHEART"
"GOOD DAY" AND "GOODMORNING"
WERE NEIGHBORS WE MET EVERY DAY.
"ALLOW ME" AND "MAY I?"
AND "HOW ARE YOU FEELING?"
ARE FRIENDS THAT HAVE ALL MOVED AWAY . . .
BEN.
ALONG WITH THE DOCTOR WHO WASN'T TOO BUSY
TO TAKE A FEW MINUTES TO ANSWER THE PHONE
HELEN.
ALONG WITH THE GROCER WHO WROTE DOWN YOUR ORDER
AND SAW THAT IT GOT TO YOUR HOME

Dorothy.
AND WHERE ARE THE USHERS AT ALL OF THE
    MOVIES
WHO FLICKED ON THEIR FLASHLIGHTS TO SHOW
    YOU YOUR SEAT?
John.
AND WHERE ARE THE WAITERS WHO ACTUALLY
    CARED
IF YOU GOT WHAT YOU ORDERED TO EAT?
The Women.
GONE WITH "CORSAGES"
AND "PROMS" AND "COTILLIONS"
AND MILK THAT WAS LEFT AT YOUR DOOR
The Men.
GONE WITH THE FREE LUNCH
YOU GOT WITH YOUR BEER
THAT YOU DON'T GET NOWHERE ANY MORE
Edna.
ALONG WITH THE BUTCHER WHO GROUND UP THE
    SHANK BONE
AND GRINNED AS HE THREW IN A SOUP BONE FOR
    FREE
Janet.
ALONG WITH THE HANDYMAN WHO SAID "I'LL FIX IT
DON'T WORRY, JUST LEAVE IT TO ME!"
Charles.
AND WHERE ARE THE BANDS THAT WOULD PLAY
    THE APOLLO
YOU FOLLOWED EACH RIFF CAUSE YOU KNEW EVERY
    NOTE
Benjamin.
AND WHERE ARE THE GLEE CLUBS WHO SANG LIKE
    FRED WARING?
I LOVED EVERY "OOO" THAT HE WROTE.
(*"ooo" chorus a la Fred Waring*)
All.
DO YOU REMEMBER WHEN PEOPLE SAID "THANK
    YOU"?
DO YOU REMEMBER WHEN PEOPLE SAID "PLEASE"?
DO YOU REMEMBER POLITE CONVERSATION?
WHAT EVER HAPPENED TO THESE?

SO LONG TO "I'M SORRY"
GOODBYE TO "GOD BLESS YOU"
WHY IN THE WORLD DID YOU ALL HAVE TO ROAM?

GOOD HEAVEN, GOOD GRIEF
AND, BY GOLLY, GOOD GRACIOUS
BABY, WON'T YOU PLEASE COME HOME?
    BENJAMIN.
WE REALLY MISS YOU . . .
    ALL.
BABY, WON'T YOU PLEASE COME HOME!!!!
    CHARLES.
Those were the good old days!
When I first joined the railroad
They had dining cars
And I'd spread out those nice white tablecloths. . . .
And there were flowers on each table. . . .
And nobody stole the silverware!

And now there's a standup snack-bar
And what do I do?
I open those midget size V-8 juices
To make Bloody Marys.
And what do I get?
Midget-sized tips!

I could of gone with the bands. I had an offer.
    DOROTHY. Ha!
    CHARLES. (*adlib*) I had an offer! I could have played with
Louis Armstrong. And the guy they hired turned into a big
name. I can't remember what it is, but it's big!
    HELEN. I find myself forgetting things I have always re-
membered . . . Like names, phone numbers, birthdays, etc.
This pleases me as I always remembered *too damned much!*
    EDNA. The other day I was startled to hear my mother call me
by *her* mother's name. I said, "Mother, I'm not Mimi. I'm your
daughter Edna." For a moment her mind had become confused.
I guess that happens. (*leveling with us*) No. No. The truth is:
She *has* become the child and I *have* become the mother. I want
my mother to be my mother!
    JANET.
Strange—

About the mind
What it chooses to forget
And what it chooses not to.
  ERIC.
I keep having this dream
Where I'm watching myself
Be a kid again
Back in the days
When I was growing up.
When my uncle died.

What a mystery!
Two men and a preacher
Came and shut the doors to the parlor
And I could hear murmuring
And I wanted to go inside and see
—you know—did he look any different
But I wasn't allowed inside.

They didn't feed me that night either
They had forgotten I hadn't eaten.
I went outside to play.

In the dream I'm still a kid
But I'm also my uncle in that closed off parlor
Trying to see the sun.

What do you make of that?
  DOROTHY.
I don't want to make anything out of it!
It's morbid. I don't want to hear about it.
  JANET. About death? Dying is an art. That's what Sylvia Plath
said. She killed herself when she was only thirty. Left two young
children.
  BENJAMIN. "Dying is an art". . . .??!! Baloney!! *Living* is an
art!

(*DOROTHY has moved away from the others, she is totally iso-
    lated, in a world of her own.*)

IN APRIL

DOROTHY.
I LOST
IN APRIL
A SON
ONE SON
MY SON
THEY FINISHED HIM
IN APRIL
MY SON
THEN THEY
RETURNED HIM

IN APRIL WAS BORN
IN APRIL HE WENT
AND THE STARS CONTINUED TO SHINE
AND THE FLOWERS CONTINUED TO BLOOM AGAIN
WITH A POWER I COULD NOT BELIEVE
IN APRIL WAS BORN
IN APRIL WAS GONE.
AND I CONTINUED TO GRIEVE.
(*spoken*)
Grieve? *Grieve?*
No, let me tell you
More than that!
More than that!
There is no word for
More than that!

To lose a son
To lose one son
To lose my son
To see my son
My one, one son
Become a stone
And on that stone
His name
His birth
His death
His life.

(*sung*)
IN APRIL WAS BORN
IN APRIL HE WENT
AND THE STARS CONTINUE TO SHINE
AND THE FLOWERS CONTINUE TO BLOOM AGAIN
WITH A POWER I COULD NOT BELIEVE.
IN APRIL
LONG PAST
HE LEFT HIS LIFE
AND I CONTINUE
MINE.

JANET.
I will pick up the pieces of my life
And arrange them
In a quiet corner
Beside the Blue Ming Vase
That was also mended
Quietly
One day.

ERIC. I never realized how important it is for older people to tell their life stories and life experiences.

EDNA. People feel — sometimes — they didn't accomplish much in their lives.

JOHN. As we look back, we did the best we could at the time . . . (*questioning his own thought*) . . . didn't we?

CHARLES. Did we?

AUGUST

PICK MORE DAISIES

CHARLES.
IF I COULD LIVE
MY WHOLE LIFE OVER
I'D EAT MORE ICE CREAM
— AND FEWER BEANS
TAKE MORE TRIPS
TAKE MORE CHANCES
SEE MORE SUNSETS
THAN I'VE EVER SEEN
BE LESS CAUTIOUS

LESS HYGIENIC
TWICE AS CRAZY
HALF AS CLEAN

AND I WOULD
PICK MORE DAISIES
PICK MORE DAISIES
FIELDS OF DAISIES, LYING ON THE GROUND

PICK MORE DAISIES
PICK MORE DAISIES
ALL THE DAISIES IN THIS WORLD
— NEXT TIME AROUND.

    EDNA.
IF I COULD LIVE
MY WHOLE LIFE OVER
I'D CLIMB MORE MOUNTAINS
AND WADE MORE STREAMS
LIVE MY LIFE
MORE FOR THE MOMENT
TAKE THE TIME
TO FOLLOW WILDER DREAMS
HAVE MORE LOVERS
FEWER AILMENTS
AND AS STRANGE
AS IT MAY SEEM
YES, I WOULD

    ALL.
PICK MORE DAISIES
PICK MORE DAISIES
FIELDS OF DAISIES LYING ON THE GROUND
PICK MORE DAISIES
PICK MORE DAISIES
ALL THE DAISIES IN THE WORLD
NEXT TIME AROUND.

    ERIC.
IF YOU COULD LIVE
YOUR WHOLE LIFE OVER
WOULD THE LIFE YOU'VE CHOSEN
REMAIN THE SAME

BY THE BOOK

AND BY THE NUMBER
DULL AND DUTIFUL
AND SLIGHTLY TAME
 HELEN.
OR WOULD YOU CHOOSE
TO LINGER LONGER
FEEL THE SUN
UPON YOUR FACE
TAKE THE TIME
TO TAKE A LOOK
AROUND THIS WONDROUS PLACE
 ALL.
WHERE YOU CAN
PICK MORE DAISIES
PICK MORE DAISIES
SEE THE DAISIES WAITING TO BE FOUND
PICK MORE DAISIES
PICK MORE DAISIES
ALL THE DAISIES IN THE WORLD

AND YOU CAN
WATCH MORE CHILDREN
DANCE WITH LAUGHTER
STRAY IN PASTURES
IN THE MONTH OF MAY
WALK BAREFOOTED
IN THE SPRINGTIME
WEEP IN WONDER
AT A SUMMER'S DAY AND
HAVE MORE LOVERS!
SING MORE BALLADS!
AND AS CRAZY AS
IT ALL MAY SOUND
PICK MORE DAISIES
PICK MORE DAISIES
ALL THE DAISIES IN THE WORLD
NEXT TIME AROUND.

END OF ACT I

CURTAIN

ACT II
AUTUMN — WINTER

Taking My Turn

ACT II

THE MEN are isolated from one another. As they speak, a single spotlight lights each one.
THE WOMEN are facing US. and are in shadow.

SEPTEMBER

CHARLES. I never told anyone I wanted a pair of silk pajamas. I never told anyone and I never got them.

ERIC. For the eighteen years I was married, I never liked my wife. But I never told anyone.

JOHN. Last September I spent two hours with one of my students talking about what he wanted to be when he grew up. (*pause*) I still think about what *I* want to be when *I* grow up. But I never told anyone.

BENJAMIN.
I never told anyone I wrote to Jacqueline Kennedy
When the President was shot
I wrote to Eleanor Roosevelt too
Once I got a letter from Herbert Hoover. . . .
But I never told anyone.

TAKING OUR TURN

CHARLES.
TAKIN' MY TIME
TAKIN' MY TURN
NOT TOO RELAXED
NOT TOO CONCERNED

SPEAKIN' MY MIND
HAVIN' MY SAY
FEELIN' MY OATS
HAVIN' MY DAY
    CHARLES AND DOROTHY.
TAKIN' A TRIP
GOIN' ASTRAY

ALL OF OUR CARES
FADIN' AN' FADIN' AWAY

WHAT A RELIEF!
LETTIN' 'EM GO
LETTIN' 'EM OUT
LETTIN' YOU KNOW
    ALL.
WE'RE TAKIN' OUR TIME
TAKIN' A STROLL
LOOKIN' AT LIFE
SEEIN' IT WHOLE

KEEPIN' THE BEAT
ALL OF THE WHILE
    WOMEN.
ALWAYS IN STEP
    MEN.
ALWAYS IN STYLE
    ALL.
SETTIN' A PACE
NEVER TOO FAST
TAKIN' IT SLOW
MAKIN' IT LAST

WHAT A RELEASE
LETTIN' IT FLOW
GETTIN' IT SO
WE'RE LETTIN' IT SHOW
(*dance*)
    ALL.
STRUTTIN' OUR STUFF
DOIN' OUR THING
STILL IN THE RACE
STILL IN THE RING

UP ON OUR FEET
UP ON OUR TOES
NEVER IN DOUBT
EVERYONE KNOWS

WE'RE TAKIN' OUR TIME
TAKIN' OUR TIME
   CHARLES.
Alvin Ailey would kill for this!
   ALL.
TAKIN' OUR TIME
TAKIN' OUR TURN
   JANET.
I shall go out today
And buy a hat,
I may buy two — I have a hat face.
I must make the sales-girl understand,
Yes, a hat,
Something fresh and fancy-free,
Not matronly:
"Of course not," she smiles:
Good Heavens, what is she bringing me?
I can see it from afar,
A bright red hat,
A busy-as-a-bee hat,
Condescendingly, Ingenue;
I rise and say politely,
No, my dear, thank you.
I'm not old enough for that!

   DOROTHY. I was always taught to stand for the elderly on buses and subways, and then a few months ago I noticed I was standing for people younger than I. So now I'll still give my seat to an elderly woman, but not if she dyes her hair. If she wants to look like 34, she can stand like 34!

   EDNA. Is it my imagination — or did people before us grow older — sooner?

   JOHN. It's a matter of labels. The World says "old" so some people feel old. It's taken as a law of nature.

   EDNA.
My mother was a woman
Who labeled her life.
"Clothes for winter — store in the attic."
"Photos of Venice — store in the basement."

Every summer we would go to the country
And every summer, right after the Fourth of July she would
  declare

"Another summer's over!"
And start packing for winter.

As for sex? On her fortieth birthday
she said, "Well, now, *that's* over!"
And packed it away with the photos of Venice.
    DOROTHY.
This sexagenarian's sexy:
In her singing
In her dancing,
In her walk
In the way she puts on and takes off her clothes.
But especially in bed.

Shyness robbed her of sex pleasures
When she was younger.

How lucky she lived to be old.
    HELEN.
Do not suppose
That "good enough" is good enough for me;
I thumb my nose;
I'm looking for a man
Who is looking for a woman,
Who is tough;
I'll make a dandy widow!

    BENJAMIN. One of the familiar refrains repeated over and over
again is that we should have no use for sex at our age. Whenever
I have occasion to see a doctor and register a complaint about
my sex life I'm told, "What can you expect young fella?"

    JANET.
To the Editor!
Dear Sir:

MAKING LOVE AT SIXTY

SEX STOPS AT SIXTY—
SO THE YOUNG FOLKS SAY
EVERYTHING WRINKLES
—OR WITHERS AWAY

THAT MAY BE TRUE
FOR SOME OF YOU

WHO REACHED YOUR PEAK
AT TWENTY-TWO
(But let me tell you something.)
SHED NO TEARS
FOR THE PASSING YEARS
CAUSE THE HEAT OF PASSION'S STILL AGLOW
MAKING LOVE AT SIXTY

MAKING LOVE AT SIXTY
MAKING LOVE AT SIXTY IS
BETTER THAN YOU KNOW

YES MY DEARS
WE ARE SHIFTING GEARS
CAUSE THE MOTOR RUNS A LITTLE SLOW
BUT MAKING LOVE AT SIXTY

MAKING LOVE AT SIXTY
MAKING LOVE AT SIXTY
IS BETTER THAN YOU KNOW

SAME SWEET LONGINGS
STILL OCCUR
ME FOR HIM, HIM FOR HER
SAME OLD HUNGER MAKES A STIR

IF YOU DID IT, YOU STILL DO IT
IF YOU DIDN'T, WELL, HON, YOU BLEW IT

GIVE THREE CHEERS
FOR THE PASSING YEARS
MOTHER NATURE'S NEVER MARKING TIME
MAKING LOVE AT SIXTY
MAKING LOVE AT SIXTY
MAKING LOVE AT SIXTY
WILL FIND YOU IN YOUR PRIME
   CHARLES.
TWICE A MONTH OR TWICE A DAY
IT'S TERRIFIC EITHER WAY
   BENJAMIN.
IN SUMMATION, MAY WE SAY—

ALL.
IF YOU DID IT, YOU STILL DO IT
IF YOU DIDN'T
JANET.
WELL GET DOWN TO IT!
ALL.
SEX APPEARS
TO GO ON FOR YEARS
FATHER TIME HE NEVER DRAWS THE LINE
MAKING LOVE AT SIXTY
MAKING LOVE AT SEVENTY
MAKING LOVE AT EIGHTY
OR EVEN EIGHTY NINE

MAKING LOVE AT SIXTY
MAKING LOVE AT NINETY
JANET.
NINETY? Well, why not?
ALL.
MAKING LOVE AT ANY AGE
IS OH,
SO. . . .
FINE!

OCTOBER

ERIC. I was never able to retire. Of course I never had a nine to five job to retire from. What is retirement like? Does it age you? Or does it come as a relief?

JOHN.
Retirement is such a nice word
For such a nasty feeling.
Canned is more like it.
Fired is what it's like
Useless is what it's saying.
I would pick up the phone to call a colleague
And wonder was I taking up too much time?
Was I talking too much?

And then I stopped calling.

BENJAMIN. I cannot imagine not working. Work is the energy that sustains life. Not working is like losing life itself.

CHARLES. All my life I've waited to retire. You know, saving up my social security so I could live easy. Working? I'll tell you what ain't working. It's the *Social Security* that ain't working.

JANET. I remember my husband's retirement. He was absolutely blissful. Time was his to do with what he wanted . . . when he wanted . . . how he wanted. Of course, he *chose* to retire.

HELEN. My father, at the time of my birth, was an astonishing 70. He was 76 when the tenth child in my family was born. After my mother's death he was provider, teacher, housekeeper and cook. In those years when we were growin up — motherless — I can remember him standing like a white-bearded patriarch, a sort of year-round Santa Claus, ironing the starched white dresses of his three little girls so that they would look respectable when they accompanied him to church on Sunday. Perhaps the vigor of his old age provided us, his children, with what it took to survive into our own seventies. Papa died at 85 — *on his way to work!*

I AM NOT OLD

HELEN.
I AM NOT OLD!
THOUGH PEOPLE SAY
THAT I'M AGING EVERY DAY
YES, I'M WEAK AT TIMES I KNOW
BUT TO GOD I CAN GO
FOR HE STRENGTHENS
HE STRENGTHENS
HE STRENGTHENS ME SO.

I AM NOT OLD!
THOUGH SIGHT GROWS DIM
I CAN FEEL THE SIGHT OF HIM
WHO GUIDES ME SO I CANNOT STRAY
FOR HE LIGHTENS MY WAY
HE LIGHTENS
HE LIGHTENS
HE LIGHTENS MY WAY.

KEEPING ME YOUNG EACH DAY
LEADING ME ON MY WAY

HIS POWER HE DOES DISPLAY
SO I CAN SAFELY SAY

I AM NOT OLD!
ETERNITY
HOLDS NO FEAR THERE FOR ME
FOR HIS LOVE I DO BEHOLD
REACHING DEEP INSIDE MY SOUL
SO I'LL NEVER
I'LL NEVER
I'LL NEVER GROW OLD

NO, I'LL NEVER
I'LL NEVER
I'LL NEVER
GROW OLD!

DOROTHY. Where would we have been if they had mandatory retirement in Michaelangelo's time? He didn't create his most beautiful pieta until he was 83.

HELEN. Albert Schweitzer won the Nobel Peace Prize when he was 77.

JOHN. Ben Franklin was 70 when he signed the Declaration of Independence.

EDNA. . . . and 81 when he got them going on the Constitution!

JANET. Darwin wrote "The Descent of Man" at 62.

ERIC. And DeGaulle returned to power at 68 . . .

BENJAMIN. (*leaping up*)
To the Editor:
Dear Sir!

DO YOU REMEMBER? (*reprise*)

BENJAMIN.
WHAT IF BEN FRANKLIN HAD
HAD TO RETIRE
BEFORE THE FIRST CONGRESS
WAS SET TO CONVENE?

WHAT IF DA VINCI
HAD FOUND HIMSELF FIRED
BY SOME YOUNG UPSTART
FLORENTINE?

John.
YOU KNOW AS YOU ENTER
NEW YORK'S LINCOLN CENTER
AND GAZE AT THE MURAL
THAT'S FIVE STORIES TALL . . .

Men.
SUPPOSE SOME COMMITTEE
HAD SAID "IT'S A PITY
BUT THAT'S IT FOR MR. CHAGALL!"

Eric.
WHAT . . . WOULD . . . HAVE . . . HAPPENED
IF . . . *SIR* WINSTON CHURCHILL
HAD STOPPED IN SIXTIETH YEAR?!

Janet, Helen, Edna, Dorothy.
ALONG WITH DAME MYRA, DAME EDITH
AND ALSO PRIME MINISTER GOLDA MEIER!

Charles.
STRAVINSKY IN MUSIC. . . .

Edna.
PICASSO IN PAINTING. . . .

Janet.
DARWIN IN SCIENCE. . . .

Benjamin.
BRANDEIS IN LAW. . . .

All.
GEORGE ABBOTT ON BROADWAY
WE STILL CAN APPLAUD

Eric.
SAY NOW, DON'T FORGET GEORGE BURNS

Janet.
OR GEORGE BERNARD SHAW!

All.
THERE'S MORE WE COULD MENTION
DESERVING ATTENTION
BUT HERE IS THE POINT
(AND WE HOPE YOU AGREE)
IF ALL WE ADMIRED
HAD ALL BEEN RETIRED
WHERE THE HELL WOULD THIS WORLD BE?

Benjamin.
SIGNED, YOURS SINCERELY. . . .

All.
WHERE THE HELL WOULD THIS WORLD BE?????!!!!!!!

ERIC. Albert Einstein had a reputation for being absent minded. He was always muttering and puttering around with his mind. People thought that he was crazy. Do you think he cared?

JANET. I'll bet he didn't give a damn about what people thought. But then, he was a genius.

HELEN. I'm no Einstein. But I'm on my feet all day and I've got a right black shoe that pinches — I've got a brown pair and the left one pinches. So I wear a left black shoe and a right brown one. You can call me crazy, I don't care. I'm comfortable.

EDNA. Remember when they wouldn't give you water in the restaurants? Coming into work everyone was saying "take a bath with a friend." The water that runs up to the faucets in the Empire State Building. When I stop to think about it, it's like a miracle, how does it get up so high? (*They stare at her.*) Well, I was thinking about water. . . .

ERIC. The mind wanders . . . it's a wonderful feeling — like going exploring.

BENJAMIN. Like learning to play a new game.

DOROTHY. That must be why older people and kids get along so well. They're not so goddamned literal.

MY KITE

JOHN.
ACROSS THE FIELD
I RAN ONE DAY
THE GRASS WAS TALL
ALONG THE WAY
THE STRING, MY HAND
HAD PRESSED SO TIGHT
WAS TIED TO A KITE.

AND THEN
THE KITE ROSE
ROSE OVER ME
ROSE
OVER THE TREE
THE KITE ROSE
FLOATING
SO FREE
FAR, FAR AS THE EYE COULD SEE

I PAUSED ONE MOMENT
IN MY FLIGHT
MY EYES INTENT
UPON THE KITE
WHEN WITH A TUG
THE KITE PULLED FREE
I STOOD AND WATCHED IT
WONDROUSLY.

AS THEN
THE KITE ROSE
ROSE, OVER ME
ROSE
OVER THE TREE
THE KITE ROSE
FLOATING SO FREE
FAR, FAR
AS THE EYE COULD SEE

SO FREE
MY KITE
AND ME

NOVEMBER

JANET. "Do your own thing . . ." Wasn't that a "hippie" expression?

DOROTHY. I loved those kids in the sixties! I felt just like them!

EDNA. It's a pity they got old.

JOHN. I'm class correspondent for my college Alumni Review. Here's what my classmates are doing:

"Eugene Endicott writes from Hingham that he is taking the Arizona bar exams. If successful, he and Kay may spend more time in Phoenix."

"Herman Bogart recently organized a Tri-State Committee to shut down the Indian Point Nuclear Plant." Herman Bogart!

"'Spider' Webb came out of retirement to open a ski lodge." Damn!

I'll tell you something I never told anyone.

I want to be an actor.

I was a member of the Faculty Players

I played Polonius and I was in *You Can't Take It With You*
But now I want to be a *real* actor
On television.
In commercials.
I could be the friendly druggist
Or the grandpa who gets those calls from cross country.
But it might mean moving to California
And I'd have to audition,
Suppose I made a fool of myself?

    JANET. You'll never know unless you try.
    JOHN. What if I fail?
    ERIC. So what if you do?

GOOD LUCK TO YOU

    ERIC.
GOOD LUCK TO YOU
GOOD LUCK TO YOU
WHEREVER FORTUNE TAKES YOU TO
WHATEVER ROAD YOU CHANCE UPON
TAKE THE CHANCE BEFORE IT'S GONE!
    BEN, EDNA.
DON'T SAY GOODBYE, DON'T SAY ADIEU
AND "AU REVOIR" 'S A HIGH-FALUTIN' TOODLE-LOO
YOU WANT TO KNOW THE WAY WE FEEL?
IF THERE'S A CHANCE, WELL, TAKE THE DEAL!
    JANET.
NOW IS NO TIME TO SIT AND WAIT
NOW IS NO TIME TO HESITATE
    ALL.
NOW IS THE TIME TO GO AND GET!
    JOHN.
NOW IS THE TIME . . .
    ALL.
TO SAY
GOOD LUCK TO YOU
GOOD LUCK TO YOU
WHEREVER FORTUNE TAKES YOU TO
WHATEVER ROAD YOU CHANCE UPON
START MOVING OUT! AND MOVING ON!
    JOHN.
EVERYONE LEAVES AND GOES AWAY!

EVERYONE TRAVELS SOME, SOME DAY
    ALL.
EVERYONE'S GOT A CHANCE TO TAKE
EVERYONE'S GOT TO MAKE THE BREAK
EVERYONE'S GOT . . .
(*turning to audience*)
TO SAY
GOOD LUCK TO YOU
GOOD LUCK TO YOU
WHEREVER FORTUNE TAKES YOU TO
WHATEVER ROAD YOU TRAVEL ON
WE WANT TO SAY
GOOD LUCK!
GOOD LUCK!
GOOD LUCK!

DECEMBER

EDNA.
I don't mind getting older, but I don't want to be alone.
You know
I was always afraid I would die at the Automat
Carrying my tray to the table
And I could just picture it;
Rice pudding, spilled milk, broken glass and me
I always thought, how embarrassing it would be
And no one would know who I was.

ERIC. I try not to think about it, but sometimes at night I lie there remembering all the people who shared my life.

JANET. When it happens one is never prepared to give up one who was always a part of each day — the exchanged confidences that flew between one another — seeking and getting advice. Then . . . silence.

JOHN. The loss of a friend is a bitter experience, never to be forgotten. How many are there left to miss me?

CHARLES. I go to bed alone — I wake up alone, whom shall I tell?

HELEN. It's not dying I fear — I know I'll see everyone who's gone before.

ERIC. I try not to think about it, but the longer you live, the more people leave you.

CHARLES.
Albert
Benny
Boss   HELEN.
Honey   Marion
Rachel   Emma Sweet
Rebecca   Aunt Geraldine   JOHN.
Ruby   Papa   George Barnes, Class of '22
Paul   Joseph   Class of twenty-two. . . .
Philip   Joe, Jr.   Class of forty-one. . . .

James Barton, killed in action, ball player, good pitcher . . . . . . pity. Geraldine. . . . Geraldine . . . Fitzsimmons. . . . that was the name, married Barney. . . . Applegate . . . Geraldine Applegate.

DOROTHY. (*speak w/HELEN 1st name*)
Tom
Margaret
Mary   JANET. (*speak w/HELEN 2nd name*)
Barbara   Stuart Goldman
Barry   Jack Goldman
Tex   John Goldman   EDNA.
Johnathan Marilyn   Survived by daughter, Mrs.
Cynthia   (*pausing*)   Beatrice Amson of North
Tommy   Fred   Bay Village, and the late
Eleanor   Thomas   Jerome Frechtman, Grand-
           Mary   father of Myra Land, David
           Elizabeth   Nadler. Service Friday at
                         the Rubin Memorial Chapel

BENJAMIN. (*speak w/EDNA move*)
Martha
Poor Martha
Martha and *not*
Charlie
Martha
(*stop speaking 1st note of music*)

(*There has been music to accompany the Litany. Finally, all the names blend together, almost like a murmur and cross fade with the notes of the next song, IN THE HOUSE. The light is now more intense on ERIC. He sings.*)

IN THE HOUSE

ERIC.
IN THE HOUSE
SHADOWS
OUT OF DOORS
FUN
IN THE HOUSE
SORROWS
OUT OF DOORS
SUN

IN THE HOUSE
MURMURINGS
WHISPERINGS
CRIES
OUT OF DOORS
LILACS!
SUNSETS!
SKIES!

IN THE YARD
STRANGERS
HANGING ALL AROUND
STRANGERS
DIGGING IN THE GROUND

IN THE HEART
ANGUISH
STANDING BY THE BED
SO MUCH THAT HAS GONE UNSAID

IN THE HOUSE
SOMEONE
MOVING ALL ABOUT
SOMEONE LET THE FIRE GO OUT
IN THE YARD

SOMEONE
DIGGING OUT A HOLE
FOR SOME POOR IMMORTAL SOUL

IN THE HOUSE
SOMEONE
SILENT AS CAN BE
SOMEONE I CAN HARDLY SEE
IN THE HOUSE
SOMEONE
WHISPERING
MURMURING . . .

ME. . . .

(*From the shadows we hear CHARLES singing softly.*)

JANUARY

    CHARLES.
IF OLD IS PART OF ANOTHER COUNTRY
WHO DREW THE BOUNDARY LINE?
    ALL. (*singing softly*)
IF OLD IS PART OF ANOTHER COUNTRY
WHO DREW THE BOUNDARY LINE?
    ERIC. (*spoken*)
A people that turns its back on its elderly
is afraid to face them
is afraid to face time's passing
is afraid to face itself.
    ALL. (*singing strongly*)
UNDER THE STARS
UNDER THE SUN
UNDER THE SKIES
EVERYONE LIVES
EVERYONE LOVES
EVERYONE DIES

OPEN YOUR EYES
AND SEE

SOONER OR LATER, SOMETIME OR OTHER

WHEN IT BECOMES YOUR TURN
TO ENTER INTO ANOTHER COUNTRY
   CHARLES. (*singing softly again*)
OPEN YOUR HEART
AND LEARN
   HELEN. The moment you understand that nothing in life is too easy, then nothing in life seems too hard.
   JOHN. But you can look back on events that seemed earth shattering. Life or death matters at the time. And you wonder. . . . "What was all the fuss about?"
   CHARLES. It isn't easy growing up. The disappointments.
   BENJAMIN. It isn't easy watching the children go away.
   DOROTHY. No. . . .

FEBRUARY

IT STILL ISN'T OVER

   BENJAMIN.
THROUGH ALL THE YEARS WE'VE BEEN TOGETHER
THROUGH ALL THE TIMES WE'VE SAID GOODBYE
THROUGH ALL THE STORMS WE HAD TO WEATHER
WE HAVE BEEN LOVERS—YOU AND I
AND NOW WHEN TIME STARTS RUNNING OUT
WE SEE WHAT LOVE IS ALL ABOUT

I LOOK AT YOU, MY LOVE
AND IT STILL ISN'T OVER
IN SPITE OF ALL THAT WE'VE BEEN THROUGH
I'M GLAD I LIVED MY LIFE WITH YOU
YOU KNOW IT'S TRUE, MY LOVE
IT STILL ISN' OVER
HOW GLAD I AM I LIVED MY LIFE WITH YOU.
   DOROTHY.
WE THRIVED ON CURSES AND CARESSES
WE FOUGHT OUR BATTLES WITH SUCH STYLE
WE HAD OUR LOSSES AND SUCCESSES
WE TOOK OUR LOSSES WITH A SMILE
AND NOW WHEN TIME STARTS RUNNING OUT
WE SEE WHAT LOVE IS ALL ABOUT

I LOOK AT YOU, MY LOVE

AND IT STILL ISN'T OVER
IN SPITE OF ALL THAT WE'VE BEEN THROUGH
I'M GLAD I LIVED MY LIFE WITH YOU
YOU KNOW IT'S TRUE MY LOVE
IT STILL ISN'T OVER
HOW GLAD I AM I LIVED MY LIFE WITH YOU.

I LOVE TO TRACE THE LINES OF LIVING
THE TENDER LINES THAT GRACE YOUR FACE
   BENJAMIN.
THROUGH ALL THE BLOWS THAT LIFE KEEPS GIVING
MY LOVE, I WELCOME YOUR EMBRACE
   DOROTHY AND BEN.
AND NOW WHEN TIME STARTS RUNNING OUT
WE SEE WHAT LOVE IS ALL ABOUT

I LOOK AT YOU MY LOVE
AND IT STILL ISN'T OVER
IN SPITE OF ALL THAT WE'VE BEEN THROUGH
I'M GLAD I LIVED MY LIFE WITH YOU
YOU KNOW IT'S TRUE, MY LOVE
IT STILL ISN'T OVER
HOW GLAD I AM I LIVED MY LIFE WITH YOU.

(*The stage is as it was at the beginning. The air is crisp and
   spring is about to bloom again.*)

MARCH

   JANET. My, my has another year flown by so swiftly?
   JOHN. Look I don't have much time, I really want to be up and
about. Most every evening I want to go out, even if it's just for a
walk.
   CHARLES. The longer you live, the older you get.
   BENJAMIN.
So what!
If you don't grow old
The only way is to die young—
And that, no one wants!
   JANET. What amazes me is that nothing seems to have
diminished except what was unimportant anyway. But I feel so
much passion about life, it's astonishing.

HELEN.
Soon the strawberries will be in season
I promised a friend
I'd make a strawberry shortcake.
And I will.
I'll make some real whipped cream. . . .
And the hell with the calories!

ERIC. Tonight, on my way home, I'll stop at the deli and buy some fresh rolls for breakfast, look in on the Ukranian Social Club — they have good chess games there. Then, I'll walk the rest of the way home, because I like the smell of the air when spring comes . . .

EDNA. (*singing*)
ONCE AGAIN TO FEEL THE THRILL!
OF APRIL RISING ON THE HILL

JOHN. (*spoken*)
A musical about aging? Enclosed find two selections.

HELEN. (*singing*)
ONCE AGAIN TO KNOW THE PAIN
AND TASTE THE JOYS OF LOVE AGAIN

DOROTHY. (*spoken*)
I was marching then and I'm still marching!

ERIC, JANET. (*singing*)
ONCE AGAIN TO FEAST UPON
THE PLEASURES THAT HAD ALL BUT GONE

BENJAMIN. (*spoken*) Old is fifteen years from now.

ALL BUT CHARLES. (*singing*)
SPRING IS HEAVEN'S GIFT TO MEN
TO SAY IT ALL BEGINS AGAIN

CHARLES. (*spoken*) Why should aging merely concern the old? After all, ain't nobody gettin' any younger.

APRIL

THIS IS MY SONG

THIS IS MY SONG
THIS IS MY NEW BEGINNING
THIS IS MY SONG
I NEVER SANG BEFORE
THIS IS MY SONG
AND IF I WANT TO SING IT

THIS IS MY SONG
I'M GONNA SING SOME MORE
   ALL. (*singing*)
THIS IS MY SONG
THIS IS MY NEW BEGINNING
THIS IS MY SONG
PERHAPS MY FINAL FLING
THIS IS MY SONG
AND IF I WANT TO SING IT
WHO'S GONNA STOP ME
IF I START TO SING!
(*feeling a unity*)
THIS IS MY SONG!
THIS IS MY NEW BEGINNING!
THIS IS MY SONG
PERHAPS MY FINAL FLING!
THIS IS MY SONG
SO PEOPLE, LISTEN TO ME SING!

CURTAIN

HOME-BUILT

Lighting Equipment
for The Small Stage
By THEODORE FUCHS

This volume presents a series of fourteen simplified designs for building various types of stage lighting and control equipment, with but one purpose in mind—to enable the amateur producer to acquire a complete set of stage lighting equipment at the lowest possible cost. The volume is 8½" x 11" in size, with heavy paper and spiral binding—features which make the volume well suited to practical workshop use.

Community Theatre
A MANUAL FOR SUCCESS
By JOHN WRAY YOUNG

The ideal text for anyone interested in participating in Community Theatre as a vocation or avocation. "Organizing a Community Theatre," "A Flight Plan for the Early Years," "Programming for People—Not Computers," and other chapters are blueprints for solid growth. "Technical, Business and Legal Procedures" cuts a safe and solvent path through some tricky undergrowth. Essential to the library of all community theatres, and to the schools who will supply them with talent in the years to come.

FAVORITE MUSICALS from

"THE HOUSE OF PLAYS"

BALLROOM – THE BEST LITTLE
WHOREHOUSE IN TEXAS – CHICAGO –
CHRISTMAS IS COMIN' UPTOWN – THE CLUB –
DAMES AT SEA – DIAMOND STUDS –
EL GRANDE DE COCA COLA – GREASE
A HISTORY OF THE AMERICAN FILM – I LOVE
MY WIFE – I'M GETTING MY ACT TOGETHER
AND TAKING IT ON THE ROAD –
LITTLE MARY SUNSHINE – THE ME NOBODY
KNOWS – OF THEE I SING – ON THE
TWENTIETH CENTURY – PETER PAN –
PURLIE – RAISIN – RUNAWAYS – SEESAW –
SHENANDOAH – SOMETHING'S AFOOT –
STRIDER – THEY'RE PLAYING OUR SONG –
THE WIZ